is this what happy looks like?

Angelica Ashley

Copyright © 2025 Angelica Ashley Epino

All rights reserved. No part of this book may be reproduced or used in any matter without written permission of the copyright owner except for the use of quotations in a book review.

Other Books Written by Angelica Ashley

All The Girls Beau Loved

you can't save her: a collection of poetry and other things written

unhinged honesty

to the kindest man

I trust you completely.

Hello there,

This book was written as I grew in love with one of my best friends.

It is about finding happiness while still healing.

It deals with topics of love, loss, anxiety, depression, guilt, and trauma.

Please take care of yourself as always.

If it all ends tomorrow,
I just wanted to say
"Thank you for today."

/how was your day?/

You are so kind,
but you are frustrating.
You tell me to not fall in love,
yet you exist in front of me
as the kindest, loveliest example
of what love should look like.

You tell me to not fall in love,
yet you brush my hair,
kiss my forehead,
hold me by the waist,
and pull me close to kiss.

You tell me to not fall in love,
yet you say things like
"you have beautiful eyes",
"you are beautiful",
"you deserve someone who treats you like this."

Why can't that someone be you?

I wish I knew the reasons
why you decline the idea of us.
You say you have worries,
but do not explain them.
I'll keep these words hidden.
I'll stop myself from
feeling these feelings.

You're finally someone
worth waiting around for.

If this is how you treat someone,
you don't love.

I would just love to find out
what happens when you do.

/don't fall in love with me/

You were worried you wouldn't
give me enough
I was worried I wouldn't
be enough

/nonsense/

I know you now

I know what you look like

I know what you feel like

I know what you are now

/love/

I'm not pretending to be something
to have you in my life.
I'm not watering myself down
to keep you around.
You know me completely.
You are one of my very best friends.
Thank you for loving me.

/its nice to have a friend/

The sound of children's laughter

mixes with the honks of the geese above.

I wear my blue sundress.

The weather was kind enough.

The birds pitter-patter on the ice.

Water still frozen white.

I smile with the clouds

and the sun that is shining bright.

/at the park bench/

I love you

for exactly as you exist now.

No dreaming, no imagination, no potential.

Just you and me

Slow dancing in my room.

Singing in the car.

Laughing over the phone.

Your hand on my cheek

telling me you like my face.

The man without the words

trying to find them for me.

Your eyes spill secrets

you try hard to hide.

It's alright,

When you know,

You'll know,

Then you'll let me know

/those green eyes/

Did you know people spend their lives
looking for what we have?

/stop looking, I'm right here/

How lucky am I to have found someone
who genuinely enjoys being with me?

/best friend/

What do you see when you look at me
for a little too long?

/I hope it's happiness/

Watching the sunrise

From the top of an overpass

The cars pass like ocean waves

The quiet rhythm of a busy city

I know nothing about the people behind the lights

But I hope they are kind

/the overpass at 6 am/

When I was seven

I wished to be the girl

boys fell in love with but couldn't have.

I didn't think about the fact

I'd want them too

/boys/

A warm touch

A soft kiss

A hand to hold

A face caressed

A tear falls

A promise kept

/the kindest end/

The caretaker with the fears of causing harm

Let me in and rest in his arms

I showed up on the doorstep

Overthinking each misstep

Covered in blood and bruises

The aftermath of his misuses

The caretaker cleans my body

does away the dust and debris

He wraps me with cloth

Serves me a bowl of broth

He brushes my hair

I kiss him thankful for his care

He smiles with his green eyes

He says "I care for you as big as the skies.

You do not need to perform those tasks.

My care for you comes with no asks.

You are safe, so sleep, kind princess, sleep.

You are my friend, and I am yours to keep."

/the caretaker/

I became a performer

Acting a certain way to cater to childish men.

Giving them what they wanted

The men who grabbed and groped me in the dark

Who loved to watch me choke as I sang for them

I moved my hips the way they told me to

I begged on my knees for them to treat me like the star they promised I was

I do not know how to not perform

I sing, and dance, and beg for attention.

I do what I know.

I do it well.

I do it very well.

/the star/

You say I terrify you in the best way possible

My unhinged honesty is a shock to the system

The way I say every thought I think

The way I don't mind the dirt on my dress' hem

You terrify me too

The quiet gentleness is strange to me

Your casual consideration causes confusion

I've never met someone so selfless

The situation is so special and specific

It feels like something I'll struggle to find with someone else.

You care too much

I fall too fast

You caught me

We are something built to last

/I'm glad I fell/

I would be so happy
If I could keep existing with you
For the rest of my life

I would be so happy
If I could come home to you
Fall asleep in your arms

I would be so happy
If I could wake up with you
Make us tea and buttered toast

I would be so happy
If I could love you
Caring for you as you care for me

We could be so happy
Take my hand and come with me.

/a happy life/

I want to be with you

In any way, in any form

Fish swimming in the sea

Cows grazing in the grass

lovers meeting in the moonlight

Dogs playing in the park

cats sleeping in the sun

best friends holding hands in the hall

birds flying through the fog

worms wiggling in the wet dirt

strangers staring at each other from other sides of the street about to meet for the first time

/to be with you/

I don't care for a passionate romance

I crave a quiet calm love

A caring soft light kind of love

The love I missed from childhood

The love I forgot existed

The love I have always wanted to know

The love you find in kindergarten when you make your first real friend

Nothing has broken your heart yet

All you know is that this person makes you smile and laugh

This is the person I want to spend all my recesses with.

That kind of love.

"You're my friend now."

/like we're in kindergarten/

The snow slows me down

No more running to you

When my sadness makes me slip

I'll keep falling, hoping you'll fall for me too

/the snow in April/

I want to be the shoulder that catches your tears

I want to be the chest you collapse into when the world fails again

I want to be the arms that hold you when you cannot hold yourself together

I want to be the hands you hold as you promise to exist alongside me forever

I want to be the face you think of when you need to smile

I want to be the body you dream of when you're lonely in the dark

I want to be the mind you want to understand more than any other

I want to be the heart you never leave nor break

I want to be yours

/I'd give you all of me, if you wanted me to/

I know how to be alone

The tower that held me taught me

I know who I am and what I like to do

Still the leftover loneliness will always keep me company

I know how to be alone

The neglect I reflect on nightly

The two years I spent on my own

Asking for his time "impolitely"

When the castle crumbles

I tend to stumble onto the nearest neighbour

Looking for someone to see me

Validate my efforts, appreciate my labour

I worry that I'll lose myself to these acts of kindness

The caretaker takes me out for a stroll

He lets me hold his hand and we walk slow

"kind princess, you know your own soul"

I lift my eyes to meet his

"right now, just rest"

As I close my eyes, he whispers

'trust that you know yourself the best"

I woke up in the garden alone

In a clean gown and a shiny crown

A letter left in my hand

The caretaker had written down

"kind princess, if you need me

I'll always answer your call

Your resilience terrifies me yet

I can't wait to see your new home stand tall

You are all you ever needed

You are enough

Beware of those who say otherwise

I've never met a kind princess so tough

I'll await your letters

But take your alone time

Paint, create, and write

I trust it will all be sublime."

/the best things I made, I made by myself/

You're good for my soul. That's why I like being around you. You don't need to be doing anything. Your existence is always going to be enough for me. I appreciate you and how "boring" you are because "boring" means peaceful.

Peace was nothing but a stranger until I met you.

/boring/

Time will pass anyway

We'll talk each and every day

I could be yours and you could be mine

I'll just keep waiting till you
finally listen to all the signs

/so many signs/

You're the first to give me up

Believing in the lonely go-getter

The others came back over and over

Never left me alone with my letters

Never trusted me alone in the garden

Hated to see me move on, stitched me a scarlet letter

With you, I have no shame

You're sticking around as my only abettor

Knowing I don't need you here

But still prefer to sleep in your sweater

/abettor/

What are you so afraid of?

Hurting me?

My darling, you couldn't hurt me

I know how softly your hands hold cups of tea

/the kettle's ready, will you pour it for me?/

What are you more afraid of?
The risk of hurting me
Or
letting yourself be happy?

/tell me honestly/

When I look at you,

I see it.

I will admit that I see it all.

The big picture, the life we could have together, a happy one, but those aren't important.

When I look at you,

I see everything right now.

In your room, the way the light hits your eyes.

The sound of you laughing causes a shake in my chest.

When I look at you,

I see you looking back at me.

I don't go anywhere else in my mind.

I am exactly where I want to be.

/with you/

I keep finding irony in this

A hopeless romantic fell for the boy who doesn't know if he can fall in love.

An optimist paired to a pessimist.

A girl who has had her heart broken in every way imaginable meets the boy whose heart has been hidden away for safe keeping for so long, he doesn't know if it still works or if it ever did.

You've traveled the world,

But I've traveled this road

Over and over again.

You speak from experience fearful for how badly this could end.

I speak from experience hopeful for how beautiful it could be.

/experience/

Does the concept of infinity

frighten you?

When you look at me,

do you see it too?

/when you want to be with someone for the rest of your life, you want the rest of your life to start as soon as possible/

In the silence I found safety in his stare

Looking for lore in my laughter

The caretaker cares to collect

each earnest entry etched

on my face during my frantic fuss as if they were fables told throughout the forest.

/no, what are you thinking?/

I can't stop smiling.

I giggle about the conversations we stayed up late having.

I miss your arms around me when it's home time.

I call you first when something worth sharing happens,

Even if it's not, I still call you.

/is this what happy looks like?/

I don't want to lose you.
I hope you'll still write me back.
I hope you don't run out of the garden
if I tell you I'm in love with you.
It looks so lovely when you're around.

/my new house is almost built, I hope you'll visit/

You did nothing wrong.
In fact, you did everything right.

It's no surprise that I fell in love,
you were my knight.

Peacemaker, caretaker, and baker
ignored his foresight.

He told me "Don't fall in love",
I convinced myself I'd be alright.

I apologized for my heart's habits
"kind princess, I know you meant no slight.

No need to say sorry, I should've known better.
your feelings, my actions did invite.

I'm sad to say I didn't fall with you
Though one day, these flames might ignite.

No way of knowing, kind princess
No need for you to wait or sit tight

I might not know now,
there may be another who might.

Don't smother your feelings like I
You and your heart are as beautiful as the daylight after a long twilight."

/we shall see, won't we?/

When I saw you, I knew you.
It felt so familiar
as if we've had
a thousand lifetimes together.

Have you been looking for me?

I see you.
I know it's you.
I missed you.
I'm so happy to meet you.

/it's you, isn't it?/

With you by my side,
this forest doesn't feel so scary
the way you offer to piggyback
you make me seem so easy to carry

everything is changing
as we keep walking
I don't notice at first
I'm too busy talking

it's starting to look more like
an elementary school playground
my backpack is filled with our favourite snacks
and all the coolest rocks we found

/at the edge of the forest/

Falling in love
It's a risk you're scared to take
Two hearts beating the same
Words unsaid become wooden stakes

/silence is a slayer/

I might not end up with you

But you've become the blueprint

For the love of my life

/I know what I want. I know what I deserve/

You make me want to be better
You make me want to get up at 5:30 am
to go to the gym
you make me want to learn how to cook
actual meals with healthy ingredients.
You inspire me to take care of myself
In a way no one has before.

I've always been surviving
Every single day felt the same
I was fighting to be alive.

But nowadays,
I'm looking forward to living a life.
It'd be so very nice
If you could be there to witness it

/witness my life/

Is there someone on your mind?

When it gets quiet, whose voice do you miss?

I know I have no say about who you think of

I just can't seem to forget the feeling of your kiss

/hope you remember it too/

You made it an impossible task
So, all I can ask is
Do you ever look at me and see
all the things we were meant to be?

/yes, I fell in love/

Good things come to those who wait
For you, my darling
I'd wait all my days and nights
If it meant you'd be mine

/waiting for you to return/

I'll only date you
if I fall in love with you
because that's what you deserve
You deserve someone
who's in love with you.

/the things you say/

I'm asking the universe once again to be kind

Please give me peace of mind

Let gravity work on his heart

I don't want to be a fool for the muse of my art.

/foolish one/

Am I waiting around to have my heart broken?

/ask me again in a few months/

Death has always felt so close by

Any day now, I could die

If I turn out to be right

about tonight being my last night,

I'll be alright to go knowing that you know

how much I love you so

/I love you, I'm sorry/

I'm folding paper cranes again
Hoping the universe will see
I am worthy of a wish
Just one wish is all I need
Please grant me one wish
Give me one wish come true
Please I deserve one wish
Just one
The same one
I wished last time

I wish to be loved.
This time, please let them be kind.

/another thousand paper cranes/

I will get on my knees

I will beg

I will plead

I don't want to, but I will.

I will always be the girl who fights for what she wants, even if she looks pathetic in the eyes of others.

I will do everything I can to get what I want and keep what I have.

I'm so tired of fighting for the chance to be happy.

But I will never stop.

I know I deserve to be happy.

There is strength in being vulnerable enough to say

"You are what I want. Please be mine."

/the things I do/

Why waste something so wonderful?

So, we can wait for something "better" to come along?

/waiting for something to happen/

Your kisses write words on my skin

I read your letters again and again.

On the days, you visit, my house gets filled with laughter and joy.

Your presence calms my heart and brain.

So, lay beside me

Hold my hand and breath me in

Keep this safe in my room

If being happy is a crime,

we're guilty as sin.

/partners in crime/

I'm really bad at swimming,

But I love to swim.

When I've gone swimming before

I always clung to the boy who pushed me into the water.

Then when their friends showed up,

They would ditch me in the shallow end.

I have always just swam where my toes could touch the bottom.

I refused to swim in deeper water because I didn't want to drown.

The boys I swam with, they either dragged to where I didn't feel safe or they'd shame me for not knowing how to swim.

I'm still learning how to swim.

You don't really like it,

but you know it's good for you.

You swim in the deeper end,

I'll stay where I'm comfortable.

You don't do what the others did.

I swim by myself in the shallow water.

You swim by yourself over there.

I'm slowly getting better and it's nice to be able to see you even if its from a distance.

I used to be so focused on needing to be better because I have to follow the boy. I have to go where he goes.

Now, I take my time in the water.

I swim with a smile.

I float just feeling happy

to be in the water.

/I love to swim/

I'm not letting you hide away.
You deserve to see the sun.
You keep building your walls,
But I'll sit against them.
I'll talk loud enough
hoping you'll hear me

"Put the bricks down and
come meet me in the garden!
I'll be waiting for you."

You sit beside me quietly.

Tell me what's wrong.
Tell me what's so scary.
Tell me why you run away.
Tell me what is so hard to carry.

Let me be the one to quiet your thoughts
The snow starts to melt as the weather warms

My darling, stop with the walls, let them fall

Just let yourself be held

You care for so many,

But who cares for you?

The answer is "I do."

I will always be here to take care of the caretaker.

/who cares for the caretaker?/

Your endless kisses and hugs
Live in the wrinkles of my brain
Your hands hold me so gently
Your sunshine gets rid of all my rain

/mr. sun/

Everything is backwards with you
When I read books
I don't imagine us
I see us

I'm not daydreaming,
I'm remembering.

I'm not making you up in my mind.
You're better than a book boyfriend.

You're real and right there

/book boyfriend/

You are the one thing in this entire universe I have no fears about.

I know that you and I are forever.

I don't mind in what way, or how,

But what we have is real.

You are the one person in my entire life who has never hurt my feelings.

You are the kindest man.

I love you.

All I want is to be as kind as you.

/kindest man alive/

We both are so scared of hurting each other.

We are two mirrors placed in front of each other.

The light endlessly reflecting against one another.

Both so delicate and beautiful

But if our fears come true

and we break each other,

Broken glass still glitters

and we will still be beautiful.

/mirrors/

Let this time be different
Let me be worthy of this happiness
Let me feel these feelings
Free me of guilt or shame
I just want to love her
the way she deserves

I don't want to run away this time.

/Let me love her/

The boys before you
Made so many declarations of love
Endless promises of fruitful futures
Where we end up married with children

You have made me no promises.
Not at all
We exist together moment by moment
A haze of hidden happiness

I won't push you off this cliff
Despite how badly I want to swim
You're not sure about it yet.
Patience is a quiet hymn.

/the cliff/

You were the first person I wanted to
talk to after my exam.

/I think I might have feelings/

There's a cemetery in the garden

Everyday, I tend to the graves of loved ones I've lost

On quiet days, I go and sit and talk to them.

I tell them about you.

They would've loved you.

/the graves/

There is a bittersweetness to feeling happy while still healing.

You have made me feel things I haven't felt in a long while.

Moments of happiness used to be tainted with resentment and uncertainty.

With you, they are innocent.

You make me so happy that I feel sad.

Sad that I didn't know what I deserved until now.

You don't even know how much of my life is changing.

I might be waiting for you, but you're sitting beside me waiting too.

I don't know what we're waiting for.

I don't know if it's ever going to get here.

I don't mind.

You and I sitting in a tree

Waiting to see

What is meant to be

/waiting with you/

"I just don't understand how you do this."

"Do what?"

"Care so much and put all this effort into someone when it's not guaranteed that they'll feel the same way."

"I'm just grateful for the time I do get with them."

/we held each other as we cried/

One day, someone is going to love you completely.

Whether it's me or someone else,

I promise you

Someone is going to

be so in love with you

/the things you say II/

"I'm never going to forget you-"

I'll never give you the chance to.

I'm not going anywhere.

No matter what,

I'm staying by your side.

I swear, I'll be the one who chooses the flowers for your dining table.

/forget-me-nots/

No one is ever going to understand us.

We found each other under new light.
Your company calms my curious anxiety.
Your hands hold my face.
Your thumbs wipe away my tears.
Your kiss on my forehead heals.
Your embrace holds me together.

genuine and beautiful
and oh so very rare.

I'll keep you
In this life
In any form

I pinky promise
it's you and me.

/always forever/

If it never happens again,

At least for a singular unforgettable moment,

You had me.

As our hearts pounded against each other through the walls of our chests,

You began to memorize me.

The way I felt.

The way I made you feel.

The way my eyes looked up at yours rolling back as your body shook under me.

The way my curves felt with every caress.

I am unforgettable.

I am singular.

I am yours.

Tonight.

Forever.

/the temptress/

You are the first person I want to see when I open my eyes.

You are the person I want to eat buttered toast and drink tea with.

You are the person I want to kiss before I go to work.

You are the person I want to call on my lunch break.

You are the person I want to come home to.

You are the person I want to dance around the kitchen with while we cook supper together.

You are the person I want to cuddle with while watching movies.

You are the person I want to wash my face and brush my teeth beside.

You are the person I want to talk to at the end of a long day.

You are the person I want to fall asleep next to.

You are the last person I want see before I close my eyes.

/you are the best part of my everyday/

I could see you in a quaint small town somewhere in England.

You live in a cottage style home with a garden.

You bike to the shops and put all the little trinkets you buy in the basket on the front of the pink bicycle.

You bake cookies and make a shepherd's pie for supper.

Your walls are covered with shelves full of things you've collected from travelling the world.

There is a ring on your finger and a kiss on your cheek.

Everything is beautiful.

/a small town somewhere in England/

There is something so beautiful about growing in love.

The slow realization that this person you've known so long and so well might be the perfect one you've been seeking all this time for.

Moments start to show themselves as time keeps moving.

You can fight it, but love will always win.

Sometimes, the best hiding spot is in plain sight.

/I've been looking for you everywhere/

He has always had one goal in mind
Keep them out
He's doing the best
But sometimes, no matter
how good you play protector,

things can slip past you

she's forward
always makes you wonder how she got in
but she never just plays to play
she will always play to win

/she knows he's a keeper/

I know I have so much more
to learn about you.
You're so quiet about it all.
my patience is endless,
especially, with you

When you speak,
I'll always be listening.
When you share,
I'll always be grateful.
When you cry,
I'll always be here.

I know it's scary to look inside.
You've always locked the doors behind you.
It's your museum.
Take your time.
We'll learn together.

/no rush/

Two mugs on a nightstand.

Sleepy eyes still trying to open just to keep looking at you.

Quiet mumbles just to make sure you know I heard your whispers.

A soft kiss on your forehead

to say without words,

"You are everything to me."

/sleepytime tea/

This book has the possibility of
either being

The most beautiful collection of
poetry written as we grew in love

Or

The most devastating collection of
longing for someone kind to love me

/this book/

I could fall in love with anyone.

I could meet a stranger on a bus whose seat is right beside mine.

I could fall in love with them.

I could have a magical story of meeting them for the first time and just knowing our souls were meant to collide in this intensely beautiful, red string of fate moment where every choice, every single step I've ever taken has been leading me down this path so that I could be seated next to this stranger who is everything I've ever dreamed of.

I could date them, get engaged, marry them, have two kids, get a dog, build a house, build a home in the house, grow old with them, and then die in their arms during a mid-afternoon nap.

I could do all of that with them.

I could, but I won't.

They're just not you.

/the stranger on the bus/

when he takes his hat
and puts it on backwards
just to kiss you

when he has somewhere to be at four
and he keeps coming back
for more kisses
saying "five more minutes"

when you look into his green eyes
while laying in bed together
with your faces so close
your noses rub and
you notice
he still has his contact lenses on.

/when he's there in front of you,
you can't help but fall in love/

I have new moles that he's never seen.

My body is changing.

The cells he touched are gone

My body is moving

On to better things now

My body is standing

Instead of laying on the ground taking whatever you felt like giving

I remember how often I found myself knee deep in the dirt

My body is recovering

The caretaker washes me clean

My body is being

Carried home safely by the kindest man

Just like my new house,

My body is rebuilding.

/my body is almost new/

I could never sing that one love song right.

My sister said I never had the emotion.

A song is best sung by a singer who feels the story of it.

A singer who believes in the words she's singing.

I thought I had found the love described in the song.

A love that grows instead of falls.

I thought I understood the song so many times before.

Now I know that I never did

/Til I Met You/

May 5th, 2024

At 10:47 pm

You & Me

For real life now.

A year ago, this wasn't even a thought in either of our brains.

We both have things to heal.
We might just make a mess of it all,
But we know, no matter what
We are best friends first.

Do your best and I'll do the same.

/bf & gf/

I woke up this morning

and remembered that last night

you asked me

if I wanted to try being together.

You had made a list

of all the reasons why not.

Somehow, as you said all of them,

I smiled at you knowing

every answer

every solution

every reason why

then you asked me

"do you want to try this even though I'm an idiot who might make a mess of everything and I'm full of anxiety and I have all these walls up that I need to tear down because I care about you and even though I don't for sure know about love, I do know that I'm comfortable with you?"

"yes."

/why not?/

"As long as you're happy."

"I am. I really am."

"Good. That's all I care about."

/he told his best friend about us/

Comfortable.
That's the word you used
to describe how I make you feel
Comfortable.

Years of people telling me
to calm down, be quiet, sit still.
So many people talked about me when my back was turned to say
She's crazy and clingy.
A catalyst for chaos.

But yet, you say you find comfort
In my eyes, in my arms, in my words.
I keep thinking back to the past
Trying to understand what I've changed

I don't think I've changed
I think I've just unlearned the things they taught me.

My love language has stayed the same.
You just understand me.

I am not perfect.
I am still learning.
I am still working on being better.

Comfortable.
You make me feel comfortable with the uncomfortable parts of healing.
Comfortable.
You make me feel safe.
Comfortable.
I am so comfortable and content for the first time in my life.
When we're together, there is no where else I want to be.
It's just comfortable.

/comfortable/

Our evening calls are so important to me.

Even if I only get eight minutes with you before you have to go to sleep, I will take every single second I can get.

You calm me enough to sleep without having to put on something in the background.

The nonsense videos of the most random things were one of the many coping mechanisms I learned as a child growing up in a house either filled with silence or things you can't fall asleep to.

I never could sit in silence.

Even in my own mind, I always seem to have something going on.

When I am with you, in person or over the phone, looking into your green eyes quiets it all in a way that I find safety in the silence.

You make my world quiet down.

You make me feel safe enough to sleep in the silence.

/I found safety in your silence/

They say

"find someone who loves you like it's breathing."

But

My anxiety makes my chest tight, my lungs hurt, and my throat closes up.

I grew up around smokers and I have this cough I can't seem to kick.

Sometimes, my ribs decide to feel as if I've been stabbed in both my sides.

Loving you

is so much easier than breathing.

/breathing/

I've been hunted and hurt.

I've soothed my slayers as they stated their sins still stabbing me in my back.

My skin is stained with blood and marked with scars.

I've fought to hold onto people who wanted nothing to do with me.

I'm so tired of convincing people to stay.

I've done my best to wash the red out of my dress.

I've stitched up all my wounds.

I hope the right people will come visit once my house is done.

I hope they will stay with me forever.

/my home will be filled with love and happiness/

I have a best friend who is the strongest man I know.

He lives far from me,

We hadn't talked in a while,

but our love never died down.

Next time, I get to see him,

You can trust I will be jumping into his arms with no question.

I will hug him so tightly

and tell him how proud I am of him.

He holds so much on those broad shoulders of his.

He walks through the mud and feels himself get stuck and instead of getting himself out, he helps other cross.

I wish he could give himself a break,

But he will always refuse.

So, I'll send him letters

and I'll do my best

to help him how I can.

He may be tall and big and strong,

But his heart is his strongest muscle.

He deserves the world,

But he shouldn't have to carry it on his shoulders.

/dylan/

The caretaker does nothing but care
I watch him exist and my head tilts
With every good deed he does
I fall more and more in love.

/a good man makes it easy to fall/

"am I enough?"

                "you are everything."

/everything/

let him be the one

let him be the one

let him be the one

let him be the one

let him be the one

let him be the one

let him be the one

let him be the one

let him be the one

let him be the one

let him be the one

let him be the one

please, let him be the one

/I looked to the sky and begged/

It's strange to feel happy while still healing from wounds so deep.

I laugh and it still hurts sometimes.

He smiles and I can't help but wonder

If he'll hurt me the same way you did.

I try not to think about it,

But when the heart is still forming the scars,

It aches and itches with questions.

Why couldn't you care about me the way he does?

Why didn't you listen to me when I asked for all the things he provides with no question?

Why is everything you found so difficult so easy for him?

He isn't even in love with me.

Yet he answers all my texts and calls

Yet he gives me his time and attention and actually enjoys my company

Yet he looks at me like I'm the most intricate piece of art in a gallery

He tells me everyday how beautiful I am without being asked to

He tells me that he is so lucky to have me in his life as he wraps himself around me.

He is always holding me in one way or another

By my hand, by my face, by my waist

He is everything I've been dreaming of

He is everything I wanted you to be.

/he isn't even in love with me/

Can a broken heart learn to beat for someone new?

She's still healing

She found kindness and comfort in you

When someone treats her like she's never been treated before,

What else was she to do?

/why, of course, she fell for you/

We are just two people looking at each other confused

Both of us amazed that we managed to get the other.

/out of my league/

I tried to burn down the new house

She took my matches away

My guardian angel, my forever girl

We sat on the stairs and she held my hand and reminded me how often I prayed for someone like you to show up.

She reminded me how long it took to build this new house.

It's not fair for me to destroy it, when it isn't just mine anymore.

She reminded me that I built not only for me to live here, but for all the people I love to have a place to visit and rest and be happy.

I got so scared that no one would want to stay that I wanted to burn it all down, but how can they stay without a place to stay?

Why do I get to decide who stays and who doesn't?

I don't get any choice in that actually.

What I can do is take care of myself and my new home.

Build new shelves for all the nice things people will bring when they visit.

Even if they aren't meant to stay forever, they will always leave something behind for me to cherish.

Even if things end sadly, I know that I love madly and no one can change that about me.

I will let people in and I will let them leave just as easily.

This new garden has no locks on the gate.

I welcome visitors new and familiar.

And those who leave, if you never return, I will always remember the time you spent in the garden with me and I will always remember how beautiful the sunset looked sitting by your side.

/the sun will rise on us again, just maybe not together/

No matter how tired you are,
You always smile at me
Whether it's early in the morning
Or the middle of the night,
I look at your face and there it is

/that smile/

I'll never leave you alone
If for any reason,
Life takes us away from each other
Know that I'll always find my way back
My one ask from you

Just be in my life

/never become a stranger/

I see us sitting together

On a bench in the park.

Two birds walk past

I say "us"

You look at me with those green eyes

You smile softly and nod in agreement

We hold each other's hand

We think about everything that brought us here.

You are my forever person.

No matter what

You are in my life.

You are my best friend.

You are the love of my life.

/us in every universe/

I let you go now

You were the last piece of thread

Holding me to the past.

I let you go now

My love for you lives in a glass jar

On a shelf in my new home

I will forever be grateful for the love you gave me while you were here.

Without you, I never would have met him.

You helped build the path to this new garden.

I wish you understood me.

I never expected to hear those words from you.

I never expected to see you go away.

Your name will forever exist in my work.

I will never forget.

/one day, I might forgive/

While walking with the caretaker from his house to mine, I felt him behind me. I felt his presence following us from a distance. I didn't mean to, but my grip loosened while holding the caretaker's hand. I felt myself drawn backward. I know I shouldn't look back, but I see his silhouette in my periphery. I can feel his breath on my neck. I can feel his hands on my waist moving down while he whispers "I know what you want." I DON'T WANT THAT! I never wanted that. I never wanted that to happen. I want things to be different. I want it to be gone. I want him to be gone. I don't want to feel him. I don't want this. I don't want this. I don't want this. I don't want this anymore. TAKE IT AWAY! TAKE IT ALL AWAY! LET ME BE HAPPY FOR ONCE!

GO AWAY! GO AWAY! GO AWAY!

I want things to be better.

I just want to be happy.

Why can't I just be happy?

/he haunts my narrative/

This story took its time

Others may start to chime

Saying we were in a rush

They don't know that you knew all my tangles before you picked up the brush.

You found me in the tower before it fell

Once I left, you were one of the first I wanted to tell.

I kept showing up to knock on your door.

You still take care of me the same as before.

I was searching for a new place to stay.

You held my hand and we wandered around for a day

I found my home in the garden of your flowers.

Forever we'll stay, we'll make this place ours.

/home/

If you ever tire of me,
Lay down and sleep on my lap
Please just stay with me

I can handle the quiet,
I couldn't handle you being gone
Please just stay with me.

If you ever want to run,
Take me with you wherever you go

Please just let me stay with you

/with you, that's where I want to be/

You gifted me a pot of dirt

A beautifully thrown piece of clay filled with the earth's finest.

You told me to take care of it.

Water the dirt.

Show it to the sun.

Talk to it everyday.

Never lie. Tell it everything on your mind.

I do all those things.

I hope and pray everyday that something will appear, but nothing so far.

I don't know what it is.

I have no clue what you've given me.

I have no idea how long it will take.

I don't mind the unknown.

I like the dirt.

I feel so happy each day I get to take care of the dirt, I wake up and I water it and I put out in the sun and I talk to it every night about everything that crosses my mind.

Each time you visit, you smile so wide looking at this pot of dirt in the sun.

"do you see it?"

"see what?"

"there's something here."

"where is it? I can't see it."

"just give it time."

Something wonderful is growing here.

/it's only been a week/

I keep dreaming of being in the car

I am eight years old

In my booster seat

Looking out the window

The mountains are so beautiful

As we drive through their curves

My hair is up in a ponytail that's a little bit too tight.

Open Season plays on my portable DVD player

My teddy bear rests on my chest like a newborn baby.

I kiss his forehead.

My mom is laughing really hard at a joke her boyfriend said.

I have the same laugh.

I fall asleep as she drives.

I wake up in my bed.

No one has carried me here.

I am twenty one years old.

/I dream about how my mom used to laugh/

Watching my boyfriend play soccer

Sitting with my best friend making silly jokes

Pointing out every dog that walks by

It's a cloudy day but it's not cold

My laugh is so loud

He probably hears it from across the field.

It doesn't matter.

It's a Tuesday night.

We're the only two people sitting on the bleachers.

My cheeks hurt and hers do too.

The game is over.

I kiss him on the field like in the movies.

/I like having them in my life/

My clean slate

Became an empty notebook

That I began to fill with poetry

/you made me want to write, in a good way/

I don't believe it is possible for me to not feel lonely.

I fear that it's built into my DNA.

There's a theory that when a baby grows in a womb it can tell when if a baby was previously growing in there. There is leftover DNA from the baby before you that becomes part of you along with all the stuff you already get from your parents.

The baby that was in my mother's womb before me passed away.

That loneliness I carry comes from knowing that I exist containing DNA from someone I will never have a chance to know.

I often wonder about if he had lived and was born, would I have existed?

Would they have still had me?

Did I take his place on Earth?

When I died as a month-old infant after being born premature, did I meet my brother in heaven, and do I miss him?

Do I long to meet him again?

If he had been born, and I still existed as well, I want to believe we would've been close.

I would've never been lonely.

He would've been on my side against anyone.

He wouldn't have left me alone.

I would have had a built-in best friend.

I'm not sure which name you chose,

but when I get up there,

I'll look for you.

/Tristan or Christian/

A dandelion is only a weed
When it is in a place
where it is unwanted
It is still a flower
And it can be loved as one

/summer has arrived and I am everywhere/

You are the person I read all my books to, even before they were books. You believed in me when this was all just a daydream. You encouraged me to keep writing when it was just for fun. When I decided to pursue it seriously, you supported me. Now in your bedroom, three of my books sit on display. You helped me through writing all three of them. They were not easy books to write. They were written out of grief, anger, and sadness. Writing them saved my life. Writing was a way to survive everything I was writing about. Over the last few years, you've become one of my most trusted persons. You've shown me over and over what your heart looks like. You've proven to me that you genuinely care and enjoy my company. You've made me feel worthy and wonderful. You make me feel safe enough to be myself. You make me feel content and comfortable. When I am with you, I know I am enough. I am more than enough. I am everything I have always wanted to be. I can't wait to meet who I'll become during this journey of choosing my own happiness. With you by my side, life has become about more than just surviving, it's about living and nothing would make me happier than to spend this life with you.

I love you.

No matter what we are to each other.

I will always love you.

Thank you for being here.
Thank you for staying.
Thank you for existing.
Thank you for being you.

/my darling caretaker/

Dear reader,

Thank you for reading my book.

- Angelica Ashley <3

www.ingramcontent.com/pod-product-compliance
Lightning Source LLC
Chambersburg PA
CBHW020341010526
44119CB00048B/560